To my mom, whose joy of giving inspires me.
To my family and friends, who fill me with hope.
And to José Andrés, for persevering and reminding
us of what we can be to one another.
—E.F.

To my Chefcito, the love of my life, Alejandro
—P.E.

**A donation was made to World Central Kitchen
upon publication of this book.**

Text copyright © 2024 by Erin Frankel
Jacket art and interior illustrations copyright © 2024 by Paola Escobar

Visit us on the Web! rhcbooks.com

Educators and librarians, for a variety of teaching tools, visit us at RHTeachersLibrarians.com

Library of Congress Cataloging-in-Publication Data
Names: Frankel, Erin, author. | Escobar, Paola, illustrator.
Title: A plate of hope: the inspiring story of chef José Andrés and World Central Kitchen / Erin Frankel; [illustrated by] Paola Escobar.
Description: First edition. | New York: Random House Studio, [2024] | Audience: Ages 3–7 | Audience: Grades K–1
Summary: "A biography about chef José Andrés, who, through his World Central Kitchen organization,
is fulfilling a vision to feed people in need all over the world" —Provided by publisher.
Identifiers: LCCN 2023016379 (print) | LCCN 2023016380 (ebook) | ISBN 978-0-593-38057-4 (trade)
ISBN 978-0-593-38058-1 (lib. bdg.) | ISBN 978-0-593-38059-8 (ebook)
Subjects: LCSH: Andrés, José, 1969– | Cooks—United States—Biography—Juvenile literature. | Food relief—Juvenile literature.
Hunger—Prevention—Juvenile literature. | World Central Kitchen—Juvenile literature.
Classification: LCC TX649.A529 F73 2023 (print) | LCC TX649.A529 (ebook) | DDC 641.5092—dc23/eng/20230417

The illustrations for this book were rendered digitally.
The text of this book is set in 14-point Macklin Text Medium.
Interior design by Paula Baver

MANUFACTURED IN CHINA
10 9 8 7 6 5 4 3 2 1
First Edition

A PLATE OF HOPE

THE INSPIRING STORY OF CHEF
JOSÉ ANDRÉS
AND WORLD CENTRAL KITCHEN

written by
ERIN FRANKEL

illustrated by
PAOLA ESCOBAR

RANDOM HOUSE STUDIO
NEW YORK

*N*o es solo el arroz.

A paella is so much more than just rice.

Especially if it is Sunday in Spain

And you are a boy and your name is

JOSÉ ANDRÉS

And you are gathering the wood

   that will make the fire

That will cook the paella just right

That will feed a few . . . or many.

ALL are welcome.

It isn't just the rice

Or the sizzling olive oil

Or the mounds of chopped fresh vegetables

Or the sweet smell of saffron as it paints the paella gold.

It's the adding, mixing, tasting, waiting. . . .

It's the spoon his father holds.

Everyone wants to cook, but you have the most

important job, José's father reminds him.

You have to keep the wood burning just right.

But José wanted to do more.

He wanted to create the magic of his mother's flan,

The smooth creamy pudding with the burnt crispy bits on top.

No era solo un postre.

For her, and now for José, it wasn't just a dessert; it was a memory
    of Asturias, Spain, where José was born.

José closed his eyes as the cool spoonful of flan told a story
    to his senses.

When José went to cooking school, he thought about

   the stories that *he* wanted to tell with food.

He thought about *los mercados* and the magic he could create

   with the seeds of ripe tomatoes and pomegranates,

   with the almonds and the cheese.

He thought of POSSIBILITIES.

Sometimes José's imagination took him beyond the kitchen

   to faraway places.

But he longed for the world in his mind to be real.

When the chance finally came, José took it—*¡sí!*

No era solo un barco. It wasn't just a boat where José cooked for a year.

It was a famous Spanish navy ship that traveled the world.

José fed the sailors but wished that *everyone everywhere* had enough food.

When José returned to Spain, one place stayed in his mind: the United States.

SURPRISE ME

It wasn't just a restaurant where José first learned to tell stories with food.

No era solo un restaurante. It was the most famous restaurant in Spain.

A place where the food *spoke* to José.

Change me!

I'm tired of being what I am.

Make me into something different.

Don't be afraid. Surprise me!

José listened. And learned.

One day, José wanted to be made into something new just like food.

He wanted a change.

He thought of a place that never left his mind.

And so, when an opportunity came, José didn't think twice.

He cooked his way from New York City to Washington, DC,

    telling stories with food that had never been tasted before.

ANYTHING IS POSSIBLE!

Chef José Andrés was quickly becoming a star.

But José knew that a recipe is never made with *un solo ingrediente*.

Everyone has an important job.

As José looked at the stars in the night sky,

   three words simmered in his mind.

They were important words in his new home.

They gave him hope and inspired him to volunteer.

WE THE PEOPLE

Not ME, José thought. *WE*.

Everyone deserved a hot meal. Not just the few . . . but the many.

No era solo un viaje. It wasn't just a trip.

It was an invitation from a friend to help.

There was an earthquake in Haiti.

Destruction was everywhere.

How could José Andrés help?

How could he *not*?

People were hungry.

There was much to be done.

José listened. He followed their recipes.

Hot meals of rice and pureed beans
      prepared just right.

The smiles on the faces,

the smell of rice and beans,

the spirit of the people,

the taste of pride,

stayed with José when he returned to the United States.

World Central Kitchen

José still wanted to do more.

He shared his dream to give it life.

It was a big idea, but to José and his family, it was full of possibility.

Like his recipes, it was an opportunity to transform.

No one should ever go hungry.

I want to help feed the world.

He gave his dream a name.

When José first saw the American flag, he also thought of possibilities.

The stars reminded him of the feeling he had when he looked up at the night sky.

Dream as big as you want! they seemed to say.

And so José decided to add his dream to the stars.

No sería solo un sueño.

It wouldn't be just a dream . . . for long.

It wasn't just a hurricane. Huracán María struck the island of Puerto Rico with a forceful blow beyond José's imagination. When José saw it with his own eyes, his heart broke at the sight.

Homes destroyed.

Roads flooded.

No electricity.

The country was in the dark, and people were hungry.

Who is in charge of feeding the people? José asked.

But José couldn't wait for an answer.

There was only one thing to do....

Let's get cooking! ¡A cocinar!

The hurricane had not taken everything.

José had all that he needed to start cooking.

He had a friend.

He had a kitchen.

And there were ingredients.

The perfect ingredients for Puerto Rican *sancocho* stew.

The hot bowls of food spoke to those who had lost so much.

José could almost hear them talking.

We haven't forgotten you.

We care about you.

WE CARE ABOUT YOU

José looked at his map.

There was an entire island to feed.

But José didn't see a problem;

   he saw OPPORTUNITY.

Kitchens in empty restaurants!

Kitchens in empty schools!

Cooks, farmers, drivers, pilots . . .

We need YOU!

But José wanted to do even more.

No era solo una cocina.

It wasn't just a kitchen. A stadium was now the biggest
kitchen in the world.

There were paella pans the size of the moon

And lines of cooks as far as you could see, making
sandwiches of ham and cheese.

DON'T FORGET
THE MAYO, LOTS OF IT!
IT HAS TO BE GOOD!

Three months of cooking.

Twenty-six working kitchens.

Almost four million meals served!

But to José, it wasn't just a number. . . .

It was so much more.

Everyone deserves a hot plate of food.

No es solo un plato.

It is a plate of HOPE.

Wherever people were hungry, José wanted to be there—helping.

Through earthquakes, hurricanes, wildfires, floods,

Through a pandemic, when the whole world got sick.

Even through the darkness of war,

José's determination persisted.

José was filled with hope.

And he was not the only one.

No es solo un plato de arroz.

A paella is so much more than just rice.

Especially if your name is

JOSÉ ANDRÉS

And you are making the fire and gathering the food

To cook the paella just right

To feed the few AND the many.

ALL are welcome.

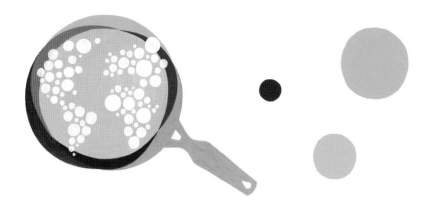

Author's Note

For José Andrés, the kitchen has always been a magical place, and José has been the wizard. By the age of fourteen, he knew that feeding others was part of his destiny.

As an apprentice at the world-famous El Bulli restaurant in Catalonia, Spain, José became part of a cooking revolution that pushed the boundaries of food. He learned to take chances as he transformed food; he learned that anything is possible.

And when José immigrated to the United States, his dream was to tell stories with food.

Now, decades later, José has told many stories throughout his remarkable career. He is a proud father, an award-winning chef, a restaurant entrepreneur, a TV personality, and a bestselling author. But it is José's humanitarian efforts that have inspired people the world over. Just like the boy who once longed to stir the paella, he wanted to do more.

José's journey from feeding the few to feeding the many was largely inspired by his experience at DC Central Kitchen, the nonprofit community kitchen where he first volunteered. It was there that José discovered the transformative power of food and the possibilities that unfold when we share our talents and skills to open doors for others.

José was deeply moved by his experience helping nonprofit organizations in Haiti after the tragic 2010 earthquake. His dream of having a global impact on hunger began to grow. According to José, he and his wife, Patricia, had a simple idea: *When people are hungry, send in cooks. Not tomorrow, today.* World Central Kitchen was born.

When Hurricane Maria ripped through Puerto Rico in 2017, José took charge and worked tirelessly with a team of remarkable volunteers to serve 3.7 million meals on the island. Throughout the challenges—or opportunities, as he likes to say—he never lost sight of the core belief that food tells a powerful story. *You have not been forgotten. You are not alone.*

AP Images / Bernat Armangue

Chef José Andrés serving food and hope to residents in war-torn Ukraine

Eric Rojas / *The New York Times* / Redux

Chef José Andrés and local chefs cooking a hot meal
in Puerto Rico after Hurricane Maria in 2017

José Andrés was nominated for the 2019 Nobel Peace Prize in recognition of his disaster relief efforts. His impact is far-reaching. Since its founding in 2010, World Central Kitchen has expanded its reach around the globe—serving more than 300 million fresh, nourishing meals in response to natural and human-made disasters.

José's vision of a world where there will always be "a hot meal, an encouraging word, and a helping hand" is shared by the dedicated staff and volunteers who work to inspire hope, one plate at a time.

As an immigrant, José thought the stars in the American flag represented possibility—the same possibility that stirred him in the historic words WE THE PEOPLE. José reminds us that together, our stars shine more brightly. Together, *todo es posible.*

Selected Bibliography

Andrés, José. "Boiling Point." In *How I Learned to Cook: Culinary Educations from the World's Greatest Chefs*, ed. Kimberly Witherspoon and Peter Meehan. New York: Bloomsbury USA, 2006.

Andrés, José. "How a Team of Chefs Fed Puerto Rico After Hurricane Maria." Filmed April 2018. TED Talk. ted.com/talks/jose_andres_how_a_team_of_chefs_fed_puerto_rico_after _hurricane_maria

Andrés, José, with Richard Wolffe. *We Fed an Island: The True Story of Rebuilding Puerto Rico, One Meal at a Time.* New York: HarperCollins, 2018.

Dean, Lee Svitak. "José Andrés Talks About the Work of World Central Kitchen and Its Relief Effort." *Star Tribune*, March 6, 2020. startribune.com/jose-andres-talks-about-the-work-of-world-central -kitchen-and-its-relief-effort/568555432

Gregory, Sean. "'Without Empathy, Nothing Works.' Chef José Andrés Wants to Feed the World Through the Pandemic." *Time*, April 6 and 13, 2020. time.com/magazine/us/5810478/april-6th-2020-vol-195-no-12-u-s

Lazo, Luz. "When Disaster Strikes, Chef José Andrés Delivers Food Worldwide." *The Washington Post*, October 6, 2020. washingtonpost.com/lifestyle/kidspost/chef-jose-andres-has-an -army-of-volunteers-to-feed-america-and-the-world—some-of-them -are-children/2020/10/06/fbebb774-f92e-11ea-be57-d00bb9bc632d _story.html

Severson, Kim. "José Andrés Fed Puerto Rico, and May Change How Aid Is Given." *The New York Times*, October 30, 2017. nytimes.com/2017/10/30/dining/jose-andres-puerto-rico.html

World Central Kitchen wck.org